Living Habitats

Heinemann InfoSearch

Living in the

Tundra

Carol Baldwin

©2004 Heinemann Library
a division of Reed Elsevier Inc.
Chicago, Illinois

Customer Service 888-454-2279

Visit our website at www.heinemannlibrary.com

Designed by Kimberly Saar, Heinemann Library
Illustrations and maps by John Fleck
Photo research by Alan Gottlieb
Printed and bound in the United States by Lake Book Manufacturing, Inc.

08 07 06 05 04
10 9 8 7 6 5 4 3 2

Library of Congress Cataloging-in-Publication Data
Baldwin, Carol, 1943-
   Living in the tundra / Carol Baldwin.
       p. cm. — (Living habitats)
   ISBN 1-4034-2991-X (lib. bdg.-hardcover) – ISBN 1-4034-3235-X (pbk.)
   1. Tundra ecology--Juvenile literature. [1. Tundra ecology. 2.
Tundras. 3. Ecology.]. I. Title.
   QH541.5.T8B25 200
   577.586--dc21

                                                                    2003001544

Cover photograph by John Conrad/Corbis

Acknowledgments
The author and publishers are grateful to the following for permission to reproduce copyright material:
pp. 4, 5, 6, 25, 26 Bryan & Cherry Alexander; p. 7 John Conrad/Corbis; p. 8 R. J. Erwin/Photo Researchers, Inc; p. 9 Larry West/Bruce Coleman Inc; p. 10 Fletcher & Baylis/Photo Researchers, Inc; p. 11 Kenneth H. Thomas/Photo Researchers, Inc; p. 12 Peter Johnson/Corbis; p. 13 Joe McDonald/Visuals Unlimited; p. 14 Bruce Coleman Inc; pp. 15, 21, 37 Kennan Ward/Corbis; p. 16 Art Wolfe/Stone/Getty Images; p. 17 Tom Walker/Visuals Unlimited; p. 18 John Shaw/Bruce Coleman Inc; p. 19 Stephen Krasemann/Photo Researchers, Inc; p. 20 Jeff Lepore/Photo Researchers, Inc; p. 23 Bryan & Cherry Alexander/Photo Researchers, Inc; p. 24 Patrick Endres/Visuals Unlimited

About the cover: Although polar bears prefer to live on the sea ice that surrounds the Arctic Ocean, many of them spend some time on land when some of the ice melts during the warmer months. The polar bear is the largest land carnivore. Males weigh about 770 to 1,430 pounds (350 to 650 kilograms) and are about 8 to 9 feet (2.5 to 3 meters) long. Females weigh about 330 to 550 pounds (150 to 250 kilograms) and are about 6.5 to 8 feet (2 to 2.5 meters) long. A polar bear's skin is black.

Some words are shown in bold, **like this.** You can find out what they mean by looking in the glossary.

Contents

What Makes Land Tundra?

Tundra is cold and doesn't get much rain or snow. It never gets hot in the tundra.

Tundra is the coldest habitat

Arctic tundra is located in the far north of Alaska, Canada, Greenland, Europe, and Russia. It has cold winters and cool summers. Temperatures can be as low as −76 °F (−60 °C), and they get no higher than 50 °F (10 °C). Strong winds are common in the tundra.

Part of the soil is always frozen

During winter, all of the tundra soil is frozen. Only the top layer thaws, or warms up, in summer. The soil below stays frozen all the time. This soil is called **permafrost**. During the summer when the top soil layer thaws and snow melts, **bogs** and **marshes** form.

In summer, water cannot drain through the frozen soil below. So bogs and marshes like these form.

During winter, the sun stays low in the sky in much of the tundra. In other parts of the tundra, it stays dark for six months.

Rainfall is low

In some ways, the tundra is like a very cold desert. Most of the tundra gets less than 14 inches (35 centimeters) of rain or snow a year. Most of that falls during the summer.

Hours of daylight change

In the arctic tundra, the day length is different in different places. Nome, Alaska, has about 21 hours of daylight in late June. It has only about 4 hours of daylight in late December. Barrow, Alaska, is farther north. From mid-May until the end of July, the sun is always in the sky over Barrow. It has no daylight from mid-November until late January.

Alpine tundra

The tops of tall, cold mountains are alpine tundra. Alpine tundra gets more rain and snow than arctic tundra. Unlike arctic tundra, there is little permafrost and the soil drains well. The lengths of days do not change as much.

2 Why Is the Tundra Important?

Although the tundra is a harsh **habitat**, many plants and animals live there.

Some people also live there and we all use its **resources.**

Tundra people use its animal resources

Native peoples have lived in the arctic tundra for centuries. Inuits live in North America and Greenland. Sami live in northern parts of Norway, Sweden, Finland, and western Russia. The Chukchi live in Siberia. These people use the animal resources of the tundra. They fish and hunt seals and whales. They hunt or herd caribou. They make clothes and homes from animal skins.

Many Sami are reindeer herders. Reindeer are tame caribou.

Other people use tundra resources

Even people who live far from the arctic tundra use its resources. Fuels such as oil, natural gas, and coal come from the tundra. People also use its **minerals**, such as lead, iron ore, and silver.

> **?** **Did you know?**
> Eismitte, Greenland is the world's coldest place where people live year round. It has been as cold as –85 °F (–65 °C).

6

Polar bear cubs stay with their mother for more than two years.

The tundra is home for living things

The tundra does not have as many different kinds of plants and animals as most other habitats. But some living things are **adapted** to live there.

Tundra is a Finnish word that means "treeless." Normal trees can't grow in the tundra. Tree roots need to grow deep into the soil. They cannot do this in the frozen **permafrost.** But many smaller plants are able to grow in the tundra. Sedges, low shrubs, mosses, grasses, and flowers are tundra plants.

The tundra has only a few year-round land animals, such as polar bears, caribou, and lemmings. But many animals, such as seals, whales, and fish, live in the ocean that borders much tundra land.

3 How Do Plants Live in the Tundra?

About 1,700 kinds of plants grow in the tundra. All tundra plants are adapted to the cold climate.

Plants have shallow roots

In the arctic tundra, the sun is always low in the sky. The ground is often covered with snow until June. So, the top layer of soil is only free of ice for 50 to 90 days. Plants have shallow roots because their roots cannot grow into the **permafrost**.

In spite of its name, cotton grass is not a true grass. It's really a kind of sedge. Sedges are plants that look a lot like grasses. But their stems are solid while grass stems are hollow. Like other tundra plants, cotton grass has shallow roots. It usually grows on land that isn't too wet near bogs and ponds.

Cotton grass has seeds that are carried across the tundra by the wind.

Plants grow low and close together

Many tundra plants grow low and close together. This helps protect them from very cold temperatures. It also helps them avoid damage from snow and ice that are blown by strong winds. Winds of 55 miles (88 kilometers) per hour are common.

Mosses and cushion plants are some plants that grow low and close together. In winter, a cover of snow acts like a blanket to help protect them.

Dwarf trees

A few dwarf trees grow in the southern part of the tundra. A 98-year-old sitka spruce tree was only 11 inches (28 centimeters) tall. Some trees grow along the ground instead of up from it. They reach a height of only a few inches. This helps protect them from the cold wind and blasting snow. Tree branches may grow only on one side of the tree.

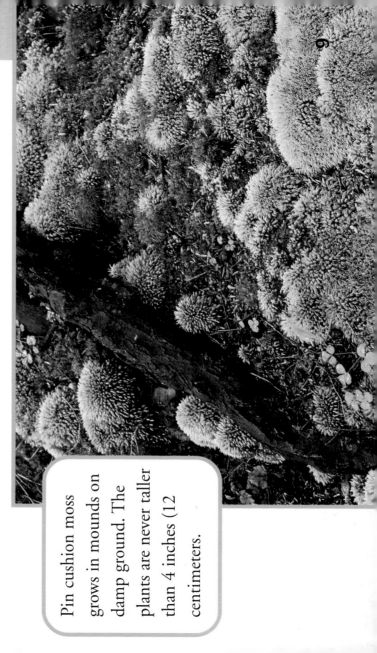

Pin cushion moss grows in mounds on damp ground. The plants are never taller than 4 inches (12 centimeters).

Many plants grow quickly

The tundra has a very short growing season. Most tundra plants are **perennials.** They continue to grow year after year. They live through the winter, but are **dormant,** or in a resting state. Then they grow quickly during the short summer. Summer on the tundra does not last long enough for most **annual** plants to flower and make seeds. Annual plants live only for one year.

New plants must grow the next year from seeds, and that takes too much time.

Most of the four hundred kinds of arctic wildflowers are perennials. Mountain sorrel, moss pink, silverweed, and arctic bells are wildflowers that grow quickly during the arctic summer.

Moss pink forms moss-like carpets with one pink flower at the end of each short branch. They bloom from June to August. Arctic bells have tiny leaves that overlap and small flowers that hang down like bells.

Arctic bell plants can live as long as fifteen years.

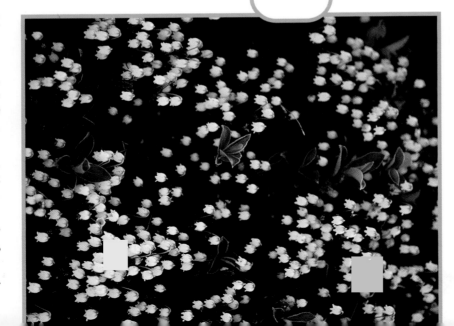

This reindeer lichen can grow up to 4 inches (12 centimeters) tall. It is the main winter food of caribou.

Plants can grow under a layer of snow

Sunlight can pass through a foot (30 centimeters) of snow. So, some plants start to grow even before all the snow and ice has melted. Plants such as Labrador tea, mountain heather, lowbush cranberry, and cotton grass are tundra plants that are able to do this.

Lichens

A lichen is not a plant. It is a **fungus** and an **alga** that live together. The alga makes food for itself and the fungus. A lichen does not have roots. So, it can grow on rocks. It gets everything it needs, even water, from the air. When there is enough water in the air and when it is warmer than 14 °F (−10 °C), lichens grow. If it is too cold or dry they become dormant.

4 What Animals Live in the Tundra?

In spite of freezing temperatures and biting winds, many kinds of animals live in the tundra. Many are found nowhere else on Earth.

Insects

During the summer, you would find millions of mosquitoes, blackflies, and deerflies in the tundra. If you visit then, you would need to wear netting to protect your face from swarms of these insects. You would also see butterflies, moths, grasshoppers, and arctic bumblebees.

In winter, you would not see insects. But they are still there. Many insects die after laying eggs during the summer. The eggs live through the winter. When summer arrives, the eggs hatch. Some caterpillars live through the winter in cocoons. In summer, butterflies come out of the cocoons.

Some adult insects live through the winter. Their bodies make a kind of antifreeze. This substance keeps their bodies from freezing, even in very low temperatures.

Millions of insects swarm in the short tundra summer.

Birds

Only a few birds spend the winter in the tundra. Snowy owls are one kind. These large, white birds have round heads and yellow eyes. They build their nests on the ground. They will search for food both during the day and at night. Like snowy owls, ptarmigans live in the tundra all year.

In late spring, other kinds of birds arrive in the tundra. Snow geese, white-crowned sparrows, snow buntings,

Like snowy owls, ptarmigans also build their nests on the ground.

Lapland longspurs, and horned larks are only a few of the birds that spend summer in the tundra. There, they breed and raise their chicks. Newly sprouted grasses and other plants and plenty of insects make it easy for parent birds to feed their chicks.

 Did you know?

Ivory gulls often lay their eggs on the ice floating on the Arctic Ocean.

Mammals

Mammals are animals that are warm-blooded. That means they can keep their body temperature the same in hot and cold weather. They have hair or fur, which helps them maintain their body temperature

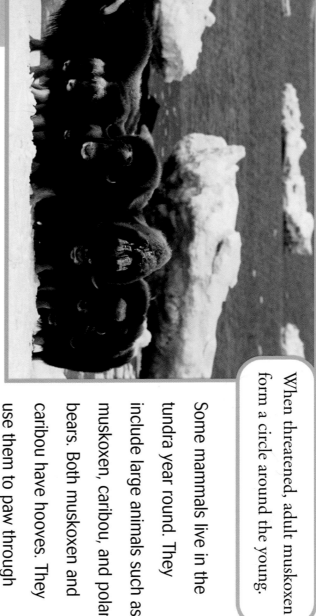

When threatened, adult muskoxen form a circle around the young.

Some mammals live in the tundra year round. They include large animals such as muskoxen, caribou, and polar bears. Both muskoxen and caribou have hooves. They use them to paw through snow and ice. Caribou can be more than 4 feet (1.2 meters) tall at the shoulder. They are the only kind of deer in which both males and females have antlers.

Smaller tundra mammals include wolves, arctic foxes, arctic hares, lemmings, and ground squirrels.

Did you know?

Female Norway lemmings can breed when they're just 14 days old.

How Do Animals Live in the Tundra?

Some animals are **adapted** to live on the tundra all year long. Others live there only in summer.

Some animals migrate

Many birds only spend summers in the tundra. As the days grow shorter in the late summer, some tundra birds **migrate** to warmer places. Then they can escape the long, cold winters. The following spring, these birds migrate back to the tundra. Arctic terns, snow geese, golden plovers, and white-crowned sparrows are a few of the birds that migrate.

Herds of caribou migrate about 400 miles (640 kilometers) each spring.

Other animals migrate within the tundra. In early May, thousands of caribou start to move north. They travel day and night. They stop only to feed and rest, then move on again. When the first snow falls, the caribou begin to migrate south.

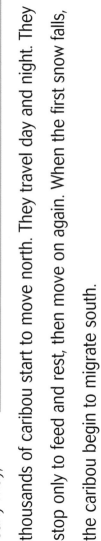

? Did you know?

Arctic terns migrate more than 24,000 miles (38,600 kilometers) each year between the Arctic and Antarctic.

Tundra animals have heavy coats

Many tundra animals have thick coats that protect them during the cold winters. The fur grows in two layers. A soft, thick undercoat keeps an animal's body from losing heat. Long, slick outer hairs shed snow and keep out wind. Muskoxen, arctic hares, and arctic foxes have coats like these.

Polar bear and caribou hairs are hollow. These hairs trap air and help to keep the animals warm. Ptarmigans have feathers all the way down their legs and on their toes to help keep them warm.

Big feet help

Big feet help many animals, such as arctic hares, wolverines, and polar bears, move around in deep snow. Muskoxen hooves are large and hard. During winter, this allows them to break ice and drink water below. Caribou also have large hooves that help them dig through snow to find food.

Arctic hares often hop on their hind feet without touching their front feet to the ground.

Some animals change color

Many kinds of animals, such as arctic foxes, are born with brownish fur. This helps them blend in with the land in summer. Coloring that blends in with an animal's surroundings is called **cryptic camouflage.** This helps hide animals from their enemies.

Arctic foxes have one of the thickest winter coats of any land mammal. In summer, they shed their white winter coat and grow brown hair.

What happens when winter comes and the tundra is covered with snow? There are few places for animals to hide. Anything that is not white is easy to see. As winter comes, some animals start to shed their brown coats. New white hairs grow in. A white winter coat helps an animal blend in with the snowy land. Like the arctic foxes, arctic hares, ptarmigans, and weasels also change their color with the seasons.

All living things need food. Some living things, like plants, can make their own food. But animals need to find and eat food to live.

Plants

Plants make, or produce, their own food. So they are called **producers.** Plants like mosses, wildflowers, grasses, and shrubs are producers that grow in the tundra. They make food from carbon dioxide gas in the air and water from their roots. Plants need energy to change the carbon dioxide and water into sugars. The energy comes from sunlight. This process of making food is called **photosynthesis.**

Lichens

Even though lichens aren't plants, they are also tundra producers. The **alga** carries on photosynthesis. It takes in carbon dioxide gas and water from the air. It uses them to make food for itself and the **fungus** it lives with.

White heather and other wildflowers carry on photosynthesis during the growing season. In winter they become **dormant.**

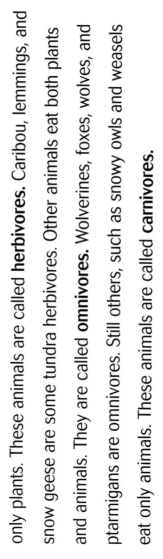

Wolverines eat any animal they can kill, such as birds, hares, and caribou calves. However, they will also eat plants.

Animals

Animals are called **consumers** because they eat, or consume, food. Some tundra animals eat only plants. These animals are called **herbivores.** Caribou, lemmings, and snow geese are some tundra herbivores. Other animals eat both plants and animals. They are called **omnivores.** Wolverines, foxes, wolves, and ptarmigans are omnivores. Still others, such as snowy owls and weasels eat only animals. These animals are called **carnivores.**

The clean-up crew

Other kinds of consumers feed on dead plants and animals and their wastes. They are called **decomposers. Bacteria, molds,** and some beetles are decomposers. Without them, dead plants and animals would pile up everywhere.

Decomposers break down **nutrients** stored in dead plants and animals. They put them back into the soil, air, and water. Plants use the nutrients to help them grow. Tundra decomposers work very slowly because of the cold temperatures.

7 How Do Tundra Animals Get Food?

Some animals hunt other animals for food. Other animals **forage** or **scavenge** to get food.

Hunting on land

Animals that hunt and kill other animals for food are **predators.** Snowy owls are predators. They catch and eat hares and other small animals. Wolves eat berries in summer. But they also hunt and eat caribou and hares. Wolverines eat plants in summer. But they also hunt and eat birds and mammals. So both wolves and wolverines are predators. Animals that predators eat are **prey.** Hares are prey of owls and wolves.

Some tundra animals are both predators and prey. Ptarmigans eat insects. So they are predators. However, ptarmigans are also eaten by owls and foxes. So, they are also prey.

Wolves hunt in groups. They mainly kill and eat young, sick, or old caribou.

Hunting in water

Some predators also hunt for food in the Arctic Ocean that borders the tundra. Polar bears hunt seals. Birds called dovekies hunt small fish.

Foraging

Animals, such as muskoxen, caribou, and hares, are **foragers.** They move about, sometimes in groups, to search for food. Sometimes they have to travel great distances to find new supplies of food.

In winter, arctic foxes often follow polar bears to feed on the leftovers of dead sea mammals that polar bears have killed.

Scavenging

In winter, animals may die from lack of food or from the cold. Other animals scavenge, or feed on their dead bodies. **Scavengers** are animals that eat the bodies of animals that are already dead. Wolves, wolverines, polar bears, and arctic foxes will scavenge. It's a lot easier to scavenge than it is to hunt.

? Did you know?

A polar bear sometimes covers its black nose with a paw when hunting. This makes it harder for its prey to see the polar bear on snow or ice.

Planning the Menu

The path that shows who eats what is a **food chain**. All living things are parts of food chains. In the tundra, lemmings feed on plants. Arctic foxes eat the lemmings.

Another tundra food chain includes caribou that feed on mosses and lichens. Caribou are eaten by wolves. All the food chains that are connected in a habitat make up a **food web**.

Living things on land and in water make up the tundra food web. Polar bears may eat berries in summer, but their main food is seals from the ocean. Some birds that nest in the tundra, such as dovekies and horned puffins, feed on small ocean fish.

In a food web, an arrow is drawn from "dinner" and points to the "diner." So producers are on the bottom of the web. "Top" predators, animals that no one else eats, are at the top.

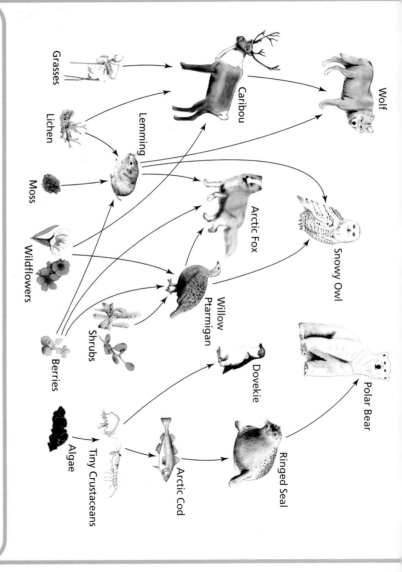

How Does the Tundra Affect People?

Most people who have learned to live in the tundra are **nomads**. They move about to hunt for food.

People live in the tundra

At one time, the Inuit lived as nomads. They lived by hunting and fishing. They made snow houses or used tents made of animal skins. Their boots were made from sealskin and their clothes came from caribou skins. Since oil and **minerals** have been found in the tundra, the way of life of many Inuits has changed. Most of them now live in wooden or block houses in villages. Some of them work in mines and oil fields.

The Sami were once nomadic reindeer hunters and fishers. Some now stay in one place and breed herds of reindeer. Many now live in fishing villages along the coast. Still others farm.

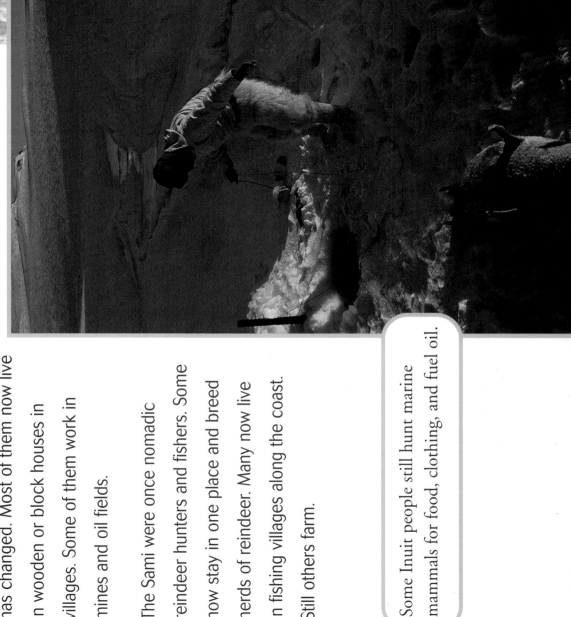

Some Inuit people still hunt marine mammals for food, clothing, and fuel oil.

Tundra resources provide jobs

The discovery of oil, natural gas, coal, and **minerals** has changed many parts of the tundra. Many people have moved there to work. But working in the tundra is not easy.

Workers at natural gas fields in Siberia live in barrel-shaped houses built on stilts above the **permafrost**. At the Mir diamond mine in Siberia, workers had to dig through 1,400 feet (425 meters) of permafrost. They had to put in refrigerated pipes to keep the soil around the mineshaft from melting.

When oil was found in Alaska, a huge pipeline was built in 1977. It was one of the hardest jobs in the tundra. New roads had to be built. Pipes had to be moved long distances by huge snow tractors. Half of the 800–mile (1,290–kilometer) pipeline was built on stilts above the permafrost. Some of it was buried under the ground. This let caribou herds migrate through.

The Trans-Alaska pipeline was built to carry oil from the Arctic coast south across Alaska. It crosses three mountain ranges and 600 streams and rivers.

How Do People Affect the Tundra?

The tundra is a fragile **habitat**. That means it is easily harmed by the actions of people.

When tundra plants are killed, many animals cannot find enough food.

People damage the tundra habitat

People who move to the tundra because of its **resources** sometimes damage it. They remove soil covering the permafrost. This causes the permafrost to thaw. Buildings on permafrost sink into the ground. Heavy vehicles kill plants and leave deep tracks in the ground. The soil that plants need is washed or blown away. The arctic plants cannot grow in these places anymore.

Destroying tundra **producers** can affect the **food web**. **Consumers** like caribou, muskoxen, and lemmings may die from lack of food. Then, there might not be enough **prey** for **predators** like foxes, wolves, and owls.

People pollute the tundra

Many parts of the tundra are being harmed by **pollution**. Oil spills and **chemicals** from mining pollute the land, water, and air. Other pollution is carried by wind, rain, and snow from factories hundreds of miles away. It enters the land and the water. All kinds of pollution can harm or kill tundra life.

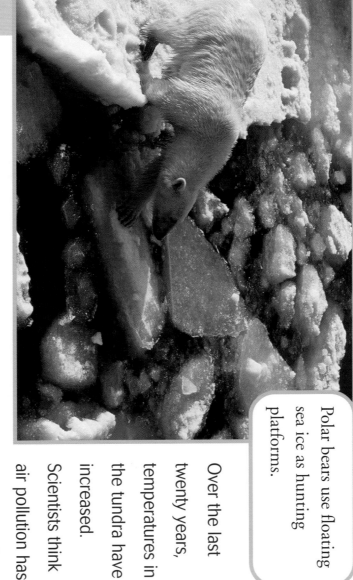

Polar bears use floating sea ice as hunting platforms.

Over the last twenty years, temperatures in the tundra have increased. Scientists think air pollution has caused this **global warming**. There isn't as much sea ice and **permafrost** as there used to be. And winters have been snowier and wetter.

Polar bears hunt for seals on sea ice. With less sea ice, bears may starve. Wet, snowy winters have made it harder for caribou to find food in winter. Scientists think this is why there are now fewer animals in some herds.

People catch too many fish

When people catch too many fish, seals and seabirds may starve. Then, other animals that eat them may not be able to find enough food. When one part of the tundra **food web** is missing, it affects many other animals.

People work to protect the tundra

Many companies now try to protect the tundra. Parts of the Trans-Alaska pipeline were raised to protect the permafrost. To keep permafrost from thawing, some buildings are placed on thick layers of gravel. Other buildings are placed on stilts. Some winter roads are made from packed snow and ice. The roads melt in summer.

Some parts of the tundra are now protected as parks. Large areas of tundra in Alaska and Canada are protected. The tundra is a hard place to live. But for many plants and animals, the tundra is home. People must protect it and use it carefully.

The Porcupine caribou herd migrates across the Arctic National Wildlife Refuge in Alaska. Part of the refuge is where the calves are born.

Fact File

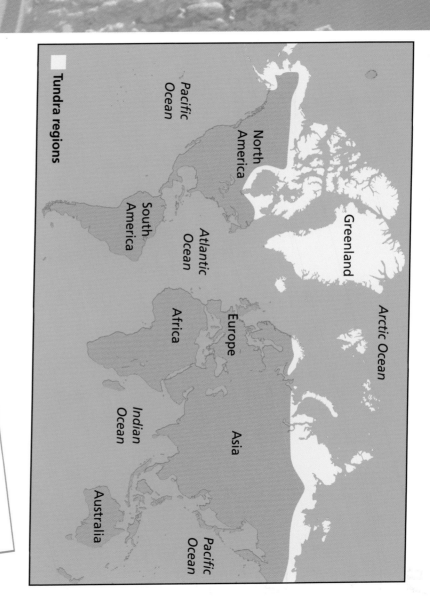

North America

Pacific Ocean

Greenland

Arctic Ocean

Atlantic Ocean

South America

Europe

Africa

Indian Ocean

Asia

Pacific Ocean

Australia

■ Tundra regions

The People's Land

The Inuit were the first people to live in what is now Canada. They were there 5,000 years before the settlers arrived. In the Inuit language, nunavut means "our land."

Today, Nunavut is a territory within Canada. It has its own government run by the Inuit people. A land claim against the Canadian government led to the establishment of the Nunavut homeland in 1999. It is the largest territory in Canada. It has six regions. A planning commission decides how the land will be used for wildlife, humans (including **ecotourism**), and resource management.

Animals of the Tundra

Animal	Europe or Asia	Alaska	Canada	Greenland
Arctic hare			x	x
Tundra hare		x		
Varying hare	x			
Tundra vole	x	x	x	
European water vole	x			
Arctic lemming	x	x	x	x
Norway lemming	x			
Hudson Bay lemming			x	
Gray wolf	x	x	x	x
Arctic fox	x	x	x	x
Polar bear	x	x	x	x
Ermine	x	x	x	x
Wolverine	x	x	x	x
Caribou	x	x	x	x
Muskoxen	x	x	x	
Moose		x	x	
Golden plover		x	x	x
Rock ptarmigan	x		x	x
Tundra swan	x	x	x	x

Glossary

adapted changed to live under certain conditions

alga (plural: **algae**) a producer that lives in damp places

annual a plant that lives only for one year

bacteria living things too small to be seen except with a microscope. Some bacteria are decomposers.

bog wet, spongy ground

carnivore animal that eats only other animals

chemical any substance that can change when mixed with another substance

consumer living thing that needs plants for food

cryptic camouflage color or shape that helps an animal blend in with the surroundings

decomposer living thing that breaks down the bodies of dead plants and animals. This puts nutrients from dead plants and animals back into the soil, air, and water

dormant not active or not growing

ecotourism visit a natural area without damaging it in any way

food chain path that shows who eats what in a habitat

food web a group of connected food chains in a habitat

forage to wander about in search of food

forager animal or person that wanders about searching for food

fungus (plural: **fungi**) living thing that feeds on dead or living plant or animal matter. Mushrooms and molds are fungi.

global warming slow warming of the layer of air around Earth

habitat place where a plant or animal naturally lives

herbivore animal that eats only plants

mammal warm-blooded animal that breathes with lungs, has a bony skeleton, has hair or fur, and produces milk to feed its young

marsh low land that is covered at times by water

migrate move from one place to another with the change of seasons

mineral any material dug from the earth by mining. Gold, iron, and diamonds are minerals.

mold living thing that uses dead plants and animals for food. Molds are decomposers.

native people people who have lived in an area for a long time and whose ancestors were born there

nomads people who move around from place to place

nutrient material that is needed for the growth of a plant or animal

omnivore animal that eats plants and animals

perennial plant that lives for more than two years

permafrost soil beneath the surface that is frozen all the time

photosynthesis process by which green plants trap the sun's energy and use it to change carbon dioxide and water into sugars

pollution harmful materials in the water, air, or land

predator animal that hunts and eats other animals

prey animal that is hunted and eaten by other animals

producer living thing that can use sunlight to make its own food

resource anything that meets a need that people, plants, or animals have

scavenge to feed on the bodies of dead animals

scavenger animal that eats the bodies of animals that are already dead

More Books to Read

Butz, Christopher. *Tundra Animals*. Austin, Tex.: Raintree/Steck-Vaughn, 2002.

Johnson, Rebecca L. *A Walk in the Tundra*. Minneapolis, Minn.: Carolrhoda Books, 2000.

Nelson, Julie. *Tundra*. Austin, Tex.: Raintree/Steck-Vaughn, 2001.

Index